Love Without Lies

How to Build and Keep a High-Trust Relationship

Marty Richards & Diana Novak

Outskirts Press, Inc.
Denver, Colorado

The opinions expressed in this manuscript are solely the opinions of the author and do not represent the opinions or thoughts of the publisher. The author represents and warrants that s/he either owns or has the legal right to publish all material in this book.

Love Without Lies
How to Build and Keep a High-Trust Relationship
All Rights Reserved.
Copyright © 2008 Marty Richards and Diana Novak
V8.0

Cover Photo © 2008 JupiterImages Corporation. All rights reserved - used with permission.

This book may not be reproduced, transmitted, or stored in whole or in part by any means, including graphic, electronic, or mechanical without the express written consent of the publisher except in the case of brief quotations embodied in critical articles and reviews.

Outskirts Press, Inc.
http://www.outskirtspress.com

ISBN: 978-1-4327-0356-1

Library of Congress Control Number: 2007931720

Outskirts Press and the "OP" logo are trademarks belonging to Outskirts Press, Inc.

PRINTED IN THE UNITED STATES OF AMERICA

About The Authors

Marty Richards taught communications, relationship skills, problem-solving and leadership at universities, military, public health and other professional organizations in the United States and Europe.

Marty, her three grown children and her husband, a retired professor of Philosophy, live in San Diego. Throughout her life she encountered a variety of situations that both tested and contributed to her interest in the theories and skills suggested in Love Without Lies.

Marty and her husband, Richard, wrote Love: A Philosophical Perspective (Ginn Press) and The Question of Love (Aztec Press) San Diego State University.

Diana Novak has advanced degrees in Psychology from California State University and is a Licensed Educational Psychologist and Marriage, Family, Child Counselor. She taught psychology courses at several colleges in California and maintained a private practice in Westlake, CA.

Diana developed many of her beliefs and theories about the value of honesty through her life experiences as well as her education and work with others.

Marty and Diana have been colleagues and close friends for more than 30 years and share a deep dedication to the practice of honesty in relationships. This commitment has been tested during the process of coauthoring this book and has survived the trial.

Dedication

Sadly, though she worked hard to see this book published, Diana Novak passed away April 6, 2007. It is heartbreaking that she died so young and before so many of her dreams were fulfilled.

This book is dedicated to her and the long list of family, friends and colleagues who loved and cared for her, and whose lives were richer because of Diana's intelligence, humor, vitality and love.

Acknowledgements

We give deep thanks and appreciation to the many hundreds of clients, colleagues, students, family and friends whose honest revelations, experiments, stories and suggestions contributed to the ideas and skills in Love Without Lies.

We are especially grateful to our husbands, Bill Novak and R.C. Richards for their support, wisdom, humor and dedication to the concept and practice of High-Trust Relationships.

Special thanks to R.C. Richards for his significant contribution to this work over a period of many years.

Contents

Introduction:	1
Ain't Love Grand?	1
What's New?	3
Definitions	4
What The Reader Will Learn	5
Chapter 1: Relationship Stages	7
Attraction: Oh Baby, I Like What I See.	7
Commitment: I Want You All To Myself!	8
Changes: Why Aren't You Like You Used To Be?	9
Resolution: Well, Here We Are. What Now?	13
You And Chapter 1	18
Chapter 2: Types Of Relationships	21
Toxic: Poison For The Soul	22
Conventional: Beautiful Or Boring.	24
High Trust: A Plan For Intimacy	27
You And Chapter 2	32
What Kind Of Relationship Do You Have? (What Kind Do You Want?)	32

Chapter 3: Honesty   35

    Why Is Honesty So Important?   36
    Why Is It So Difficult?   38
    Be Careful What You Ask For.   40
    What About Secrets?   40
    You and Chapter 3   48
    How Honest Are You?   48

Chapter 4: Communication - The Key To Intimacy   49

    How To Learn More About Yourself   50
    How To Talk About Yourself   52
    How to Say What You Mean   53
    How To Listen With Love   55
    I'm Not Defensive. I'm Not, I'm Not, I'm Not!   57
    Criticism, Complaints And Compliments   61
    You And Chapter 4   68
    Communication Assessments   70

Chapter 5: Problem Solving   73

    Conflict: Trouble Or Opportunity?   73
    Common Beliefs About Conflict   77
    Beliefs That Help Solve Problems   77
    Common Reactions To Conflict   78
    A Better Way   80
    Seven Steps To Success   82
    What If It Doesn't Work?   85
    You And Chapter 5   87
    To Our Readers   90

Introduction

Have you noticed that some people have a whole lot of trouble with love? They want it, they lose sleep over it, they sacrifice for it and they do crazy things because of it. Love can give a lifetime of pleasure or decades of grief. We've written this book to help you build the best relationship possible.

> **A Brief History**: Org, the caveman searched for food but was worn out from the hunt, and wasn't good with barbeque. So he invited Edu, a most alluring neighbor, to light his fire and cook for him. After dinner, the mood took over and Edu just couldn't resist his advances. Several moons later a baby appeared and family life began.
>
> Eons passed and because of geography, economics, politics and religion, the structure of families evolved. The most common kind now is a couple, their offspring, and often, children from previous relationships.

Ain't Love Grand?

The *happily-ever-after* unions of the 1940s and '50s, the *free love, if-it-feels-good-do-it* mantras of the '60s and '70s, the *I'm-number-one, I'm entitled* attitudes of the '80s and '90s didn't do much to improve things. We are in a new century and so are love relationships. We need new assumptions and skills while keeping the "old fashioned" ones that work.

You may be one of millions of hopeful people who thought they found the perfect person and just *knew* their love would last forever. Maybe you were even *absolutely sure* more than once. Did you promise. . .

I'll love you forever.

It will always be like this.

Love conquers all.

Our love will never change.

All we need is love.

We're not like the others.

...and you probably meant it—positively, definitely meant it.

> Geri and Marco started out with passion and the best of intentions. In spite of the high rate of failed marriages and their own experiences, they *knew* they'd have a better relationship than their parents or friends had. They were sure that this time, with this partner, it would be different.
>
> It's no surprise, but the freshness and infatuation that fueled those early years slipped to the background as daily chores, obligations and distractions replaced the passion. Minor irritations became major battles as Geri started nagging and Marco withdrew.
>
> They didn't know what happened or why, and they both tried to ignore the aching loss of what once felt so good. They discovered that hope, hormones and good intentions were not enough, but they didn't know what to do about it.

Too many people are disappointed in their relationships but can't even get their partner to talk about it, let alone do anything to fix it. Some of their friends and co-workers know them better than their own partners do.

You're reading this, so you must want to make your relationship better. We think this book will help. Let's start by listing some of the factors that influence love relationships today.

What's new?

- People want more from relationships than ever before—a partner who is an equal, a lover and best friend.

- They realize that past and current models often fail, but they don't have a new model to guide them.

- Roles have shifted. More women now work outside the home and more men are involved with housework and childcare.

- Movies, television and the internet have a strong influence on people and their relationships.

- People live longer and healthier. There is more time to get things right and more time to mess them up.

- Many children are over-indulged, overly-stimulated, and grow up with an exaggerated sense of entitlement.

- Women are not as economically dependent as they once were, so are freer to leave a relationship.

- Religion is a diminishing factor in many relationships.

- Many people expect perfection in everything, including

their partner and their relationships.

- There are more kinds of families: blended, same sex, single parent, and grandparents raising their grandchildren.

- It is socially and legally easier to end relationships.

Even with these influences, people still look with hope to monogamous, long-term unions just as they want more than just a paycheck from their jobs. They want a fulfilling and loving partner. We wrote this book so readers can get and give more in their love relationships.

Definitions

Here are the definitions of some of the words in this book so you know exactly what we mean when we use them.

Respect:	The admiration for a person's values and actions; to show consideration and thoughtfulness.
Integrity:	Steadfastly adhering to high moral principles.
Honesty:	Truthfulness, candor or sincerity.
Trust:	Assurance about the character, ability, strength and honesty of another.
Character:	The traits that make up and distinguish an individual.
Empathy:	The willingness and ability to understand and identify with another person's feelings and experiences.
Intimacy:	The deep closeness in a relationship that comes from honesty, understanding, respect, empathy, trust and love.

Now we're ready to explore the High-Trust Relationship.

> A High-Trust Relationship is a healthy, nurturing union built on honesty, intimacy, respect and personal integrity. It is free from fear, threat and manipulation.

What The Reader Will Learn

As you read this book and do the exercises you will learn to:

- Identify the three types of relationships.

- Evaluate your relationship.

- Discover the truth about yourself, your partner and your relationship.

- Tell the truth even when it hurts.

- Listen so your partner will tell you the truth.

- Show respect for your partner's expectations and values.

- Recognize potential problems early.

- Solve problems and work with disagreements.

- Deal with problems that can't be solved.

Chapter 1
Relationship Stages

Every relationship goes through stages. Some move smoothly from simple attraction to a lifelong love affair. Others go from blissful infatuation to mutual revulsion. Some relationships take decades to go through the stages and others manage it all in a quickie weekend. Let's take a look at four common stages:

1. Attraction   2. Commitment   3. Changes   4. Resolution

Most people simply move from stage to stage, unaware of what is happening. They let things happen as if they have no control. Others pay attention and take charge of what happens to them. They expect the relationship to change and they have a plan to deal with the transitions from one stage to another.

7

Marty Richards & Diana Novak

Stage 1, Attraction: Oh Baby, I Like What I See!

Remember the flirting, the fast heartbeat, sleepless nights and thinking, *I've died and gone to heaven*? You try to impress each other by looking and acting your best. You may both tell little (or big) lies. You pretend you are what you think the other wants.

I'm in graduate school, when the truth is you took a weekend extension course.

Or, *Oh, I only did a little pot many years ago*, when in fact, he spent a year in prison for dealing drugs.

Or, *You like chamber music? Me too, it's my favorite*, when in fact, she doesn't know the difference between chamber music and a chamber pot.

These lies (call them little embellishments if you want) are not usually done with malice, but simply to make each person seem more appealing to the other. The downside is that as time goes by you have to either make good on the lies or eventually fess up to them. It's especially hard to keep the deception going if you pretend to be a model, millionaire, neurosurgeon or world-class athlete.

On-going attraction brings excitement and sometimes, even obsession. You are both interested in what the other does and says. You hang on to her every word and she treats you like a king. You'll do anything to please each other even if it means putting your own needs aside. Everything seems wonderful, and you ignore or excuse what isn't.

During this infatuation phase oxygen leaves the brain and rushes to other important parts of your body. As the relationship moves forward you may think you've found your one and only—your soul mate. You both want more, so sometimes, even without thinking (of course without thinking—you have a diminished supply of oxygen to your brain), you move to the next stage.

> **The essence of love begins when infatuation ends.**
> *Unknown*

Stage 2, Commitment: I Want You All To Myself!

Commitment begins with romantic expectations. You want to keep the excitement and satisfaction and you start thinking about the future. Now you see yourself as a couple and you spend time imagining what life would be like together. You're pretty sure you've found a partner, lover and best friend.

> **Love is an attempt to change a piece of a dream world into reality.**
> *Theodore Reich*

You establish traditions, fall into habits and start to make agreements. Sometimes you are specific about what you expect, but most of the time you assume that the details will take care of themselves. Because you are so in love (or at least in lust) the important thing is just being together. This is a time you should get to know each other better—warts and all—but often, the fog of infatuation rules.

You are now a couple. Your life is active and satisfying. You talk for hours. You touch, kiss and snuggle. You can't get enough of each other but you try. The sexual tension is sometimes overwhelming. You start talking about moving in together, getting married, or plan to get matching tattoos.

At this stage you assume that your enthusiasm is enough to keep love alive and vibrant. You are so satisfied that you hope, and maybe expect, that everything will stay the same. But every one and every thing changes. You make promises that you will not, never in a million years, be able to keep.

I could spend every Saturday just watching you play tennis.

I'll get up every morning to make your breakfast.

In sickness and health, for better or worse, for richer or poorer.

I'll make love with you anytime, anyplace.

I won't let the baby affect our relationship.

You can handle the finances...I trust your judgment completely.

Nothing is permanent but change.

Heraclitus, 5th Century, B.C.

However, time passes and stuff happens. The relationship will move to the next stage.

Stage 3, Changes: Why Aren't You Like You Used To Be?

You start seeing each other's imperfections. Some of what you used to think of as charming, cute or idiosyncratic now becomes downright irritating. You didn't expect it, you don't like it, but you've got it. You look back at those old promises and think…

Oh, no—not tennis again!

I'm too tired to make your breakfast. I need to sleep.

I wish you'd get a better job. You just don't make enough money.

Sex, again? Can't you give it a rest?

I'm going crazy. I just can't manage my work, this house and the baby!

I'll take care of the finances. You're ruining us.

> **It is the nature of a man, as he grows older, a small bridge in time, to protest against change, particularly change for the better.**
>
> *John Steinbeck*

Some people deal well with this stage. They accept the inevitable changes as part of life and face them with enthusiasm. They keep communication open and resolve differences, problems and conflicts as they come along. When you deal well with this stage, you increase the excitement and satisfaction. The important thing is that you talk about what's happening, see the changes as opportunities to increase intimacy, then find ways to improve your lives.

Other couples are surprised by the changes and have a hard

time adjusting to them. They might see change as a threat to the relationship and they might be right. They can ignore them for a while and hope that some *magic* event or just the passing of time will return the relationship to its happier state. But now, unless they do something drastic and positive, they start blaming or trying to change each other, hoping that with just a few minor adjustments (preferably on the part of their partner), everything will be fine again.

They might complain to friends, or even strangers, and refer to the relationship as a burden; *My old lady…, She won't let me…, 'Gotta check with the warden…, Thank goodness he's going out of town for a week.*

> **Unless someone like you cares a whole awful lot, nothing is going to get better. It's not.**
> *Dr. Seuss*

If you don't handle changes well, you'll have problems and some of them will be big ones. Changes often turn into crises that are much harder to solve. This is when you get cranky, pout, blame, argue, cry, nag or withdraw. Anger, resentment and guilt replace the tenderness and consideration that once marked the relationship. Sometimes, heaven forbid, you even go out of your way to irritate each other. You might try to ignore your difficulties and differences. Sad but true. At this stage, and without good communication and negotiation skills, few people work through their problems without professional help.

> The truth is that our finest moments are most likely to occur when we are feeling deeply uncomfortable, unhappy, or unfulfilled. For it is only in such moments, propelled by our discomfort, that we are likely to step out of our ruts and start searching for different ways or truer answers.
>
> *M. Scott Peck*

Stage 4, Resolution: Well, Here We Are. What Now?

This is the stage when you decide as a couple how to spend the rest your lives. If you dealt well during the first three stages you will probably do well in this one. This is a good time to take a look at things and make some important decisions. Ask yourself these questions:

Do you both accept that infatuation is temporary and the *everything's wonderful* phase will not last?

How well do you handle your changes, differences and conflicts?

How honest are you with yourself and each other?

How well do you solve problems as they come up?

How deep is the trust and closeness between the two of you?

How important to you is your partner's happiness?

How important is your happiness to your partner?

How important is your own happiness to you?

Do you treat each other with respect and kindness?

Do you have fun together and see each other as best friends?

Do you spend enough time and energy keeping your relationship a high priority?

In short: How satisfied are you with the life you have together?

After you answer these questions honestly, think about what to do with your relationship. There are four basic options.

1. Stay together and have a satisfying life.

2. Stay together and live unhappily ever after.

3. End the relationship with civility and cooperation.

4. End the relationship with anger, blame and resentment.

Let's take a look at each of these options.

1. Stay together and live a mutually satisfying life.

At its best, the relationship becomes comfortable and rewarding. The partners accept or adjust to their differences, and they are good at solving problems without producing resentment. They know each other well and are lovers, companions and friends. They are still excited to learn about each other, and they work to keep the relationship healthy. They accept that their drives and abilities slow down as time passes but they remain physically involved and continue to please each other with frequent touching, loving words and thoughtful gestures.

2. Stay together and live unhappily ever after.

Some couples give up trying to make the relationship better. They establish some kind of truce and simply become roommates. They share the house and the chores, and sometimes even try to present themselves as a model of contentment. Some couples don't even try. You may have seen them out in public, rarely talking or even making eye contact. They often turn to other people or activities for excitement because their lives together are so unrewarding.

Some stay together out of habit. They are used to each other and don't want to go through the inconvenience, pain or embarrassment of breaking up. They are resigned to a life of mutually agreeable incompatibility. Some stay together out of fear, dependence or lack of self-confidence.

3. End the relationship with respect and concern for each other.

Sometimes the relationship just runs its course. There's little or no anger or resentment, just an agreement that one or both partners want out. Maybe values or priorities changed and they decide that living apart would be best for both of them. They put their differences and egos aside. They continue to use good communication and problem-solving skills. They work hard to avoid hurting each other or their children. Remarkably, some couples even remain friends and keep the family ties strong.

> Pete and Ada had a good marriage for twelve years before they *fell out of love.* They tried to revive the feelings but failed. They agreed that divorce was the answer. Pete was especially angry about the split because he said he

had done everything right. In spite of that, as well as feeling disappointment and guilt, they decided to make the divorce as painless as possible.

With the help of a mediator, they mapped out a plan that would minimize the damage. The first year was tough, but they decided they'd always be a family. They got together for their children's birthdays, sporting events and school activities. They admitted the sadness that resulted from not living out their promises and dreams of life together, but they worked to maintain the friendship they shared during their marriage. Eventually, they both admitted their relationship after the divorce was better than the last few years in it. Their children still benefit from Pete and Ada's love and lack of selfishness.

4. End the relationship with anger, blame and resentment.

For a variety of reasons, one or both people decide to end the relationship, but they do it badly. They blame each other and try to get even for the wrongs they think their partner committed. This is the pits. Their dream became a nightmare. Hurt and resentment cloud all reason, so they just can't (or won't) think straight or behave themselves. Everyone is affected and the children, no matter their ages, probably suffer the fallout from their selfish parents.

It is common that before this stage one person will try to fix things: get counseling, read self-help books, use prayer or practice patience. Without a cooperative partner, the effort to save the relationship is usually wasted. Spending time in counseling and with emotionally healthy friends and family might help. If a person accepts responsibility for his or her part of the failure, and refuses to wallow in the *victim* role, the best that a person can do is to keep a steady, responsible course regardless of the partner's negative attitude or actions.

Review

Nearly all relationships go through predictable stages. If the process is allowed to happen without much thought or planning, one likely result is disappointment. But if two people use good communication and problem-solving skills, if they are creative, respectful and flexible, they certainly increase the chances of building and keeping a loving relationship. Which is it for you? It's up to the two of you to decide.

> **Love doesn't make the world go around. It makes the ride worthwhile.**
> *Franklin P. Jones*

You and Chapter 1

Attraction

Can you remember something you misrepresented about yourself; some flaw you omitted when you talked about yourself? Or perhaps you stretched the truth a bit when talking about an interest, accomplishment or positive character trait. List two such *innocent* deceptions. How about your partner? List two beliefs or assumptions you had about your partner which don't seem to be true now.

Commitment

What are some of the ways you and your partner showed your commitment to each other in the early stages of your relationship? Do you still do those things?

Changes

As time passed and the bloom of your romance began to fade, what are some of the changes—both good and bad—that you notice in yourself and your partner?

How did you react to the changes? Did you acknowledge them, talk about them and make plans to adapt to them? Or did you simply ignore them?

Resolution

Did some of the changes turn into conflicts? What are they and how did you (or do you) deal with them? These might be minor irritations about different ways of doing things or they might be clashes about important values.

As a relationship evolves, a couple may:

1. Stay together and live a satisfying life.

2. Stay together and live unhappily ever after.

3. End the relationship with respect and concern for each other.

4. End the relationship with anger, blame and resentment.

Which of these four options most closely describes your relationship now?

Marty Richards & Diana Novak

Which most closely describes what you want?

What is one thing you will do now to improve your relationship?

Chapter 2
Types of Relationships

> A High-Trust Relationship is a healthy, nurturing union built on honesty, intimacy, respect and personal integrity. It is free from fear, threat and manipulation.

The High-Trust Relationship is for those who want to increase the quality of their relationship and are willing to consider some new ideas and learn new skills.

Let's take a look at three kinds of relationships: Toxic, Conventional and High-Trust.

<u>A Toxic Relationship</u> is downright awful. It is marked by abuse, fear, dependence, neglect and selfishness.

<u>A Conventional Relationship</u> is the most typical and is based on stability, comfort, habit and predictability.

<u>A High-Trust Relationship</u> is a healthy, nurturing union built on honesty, intimacy, respect and personal integrity. It is free from fear, threat and manipulation.

Imagine a line with toxic at one end and High-Trust at the other. Conventional relationships fall somewhere in between. A relationship might be High-Trust in some areas, conventional in others and even toxic in others. For example, a couple might be High-Trust as far as their communication goes, conventional in their commitment to each other, but then turn into monsters about money. Whether a conventional relationship is beautiful or boring depends on the level of desire, commitment, skills, compassion and time devoted to it.

Toxic: Poison for the Soul

A toxic relationship is absolutely awful—serious emotional poison. It might have begun with infatuation, but quickly deteriorated because of immaturity, ignorance, selfishness or the lack of important skills. These unions are marked by dependence and fear and are breeding grounds for resentment, anger and depression. Physical, psychological and substance abuse are common, and these factors create the worst possible environments for children.

> Kevin slammed the door behind him when he got home. He yelled for Maggie, demanding to know why toys were scattered on the driveway. She tried to explain but Kevin interrupted with rantings (#!*@%*) about her laziness and lack of control over the kids. He got louder by the minute. Maggie was on the verge of tears but knew better than to argue. Kevin ignored the dinner she had ready for him, grabbed a beer, shoved the kids off the sofa and plopped himself down in front of the TV.

Because people in toxic relationships are driven by their emotions, they use anger, sulking, name-calling and other hurtful actions in their attempts to control each other. They are critical of their partner in private, public and in front of the children. They know each other's sore spots and use them to punish or get even. They are not interested in their partner's needs or feelings, and they blame each other for what goes wrong. They sometimes do the exact opposite of what might get them what they want. For instance, one partner may yell or sulk when a quiet talk might work. They may even get some kind of *satisfaction* from winning an argument or proving the other is wrong. They are selfish and often, their idea of closeness or intimacy is sex.

I just wish we could be closer like we used to be.

What do you mean, close? We had sex last week, didn't we? ...can't get much closer than that.

The most aggressive person calls the shots.

Because I said so, that's why.
I don't care what you want. Just do what I tell you.
I know what's best for you. Don't argue with me.
I'll make you pay for this.

One partner might take all the blame and becomes the victim.

*I wish I didn't have to boss you around so much
but you just won't listen to me!*

I know. I'm so sorry; I'll do better next time.

People in toxic relationships bring out the worst in each other. They . . .

- snoop and check up on each other.

- use name-calling, hostile teasing and sarcasm.

- belittle and make nasty, critical remarks.

- lie, cheat, ignore, blame, deceive.

- embarrass each other in front of others.

- curse, yell, whine, sulk, cry, nag.

- seek comfort from affairs, drugs, alcohol, food, television, pornography, computers, gambling, shopping or work.

- refuse to accept any responsibility for the state of the relationship.

- refuse to get help.

- avoid direct, considerate communication and problem-solving.

As bad as toxic relationships are for the people in them and around them, they are especially tragic for the innocent children who grow up believing this kind of relationship is normal.

> Joey watched as his mom stormed out of the house, yelling and slamming the back door. He turned to his dad and whispered, Why is Mom so mad all the time? His dad hugged him and said, *We need to be more careful about Mommy's moods. If we just did what she wants us to, she wouldn't get so angry.*

Sometimes people in these relationships regret the abuse they give or get. They may apologize over and over and promise never to be mean or accept the abuse again, but the awful pattern returns. The best and only way to survive a toxic relationship is to get out of it.

Conventional: Beautiful or Boring

A conventional relationship is stable, comfortable and predictable, at least in the early stages. At its best, it is a practical and socially acceptable way of life that provides friendship and companionship for parenting, chores, sex and financial support. It gives both partners an extended family and supportive community.

Society and peer groups usually define the couple's roles and expectations: Who does which chores? Who disciplines the children? Whose responsibilities take top priority? Who decides how money is spent? Too few people spend enough time planning the details of their lives together. In fact, most people spend much more time, energy and money planning the wedding itself instead of planning their marriage and talking about their expectations, roles, priorities and values.

Most people agree that trust is important in a conventional relationship and it is usually defined as, *I expect my partner to do what has always been done*, or, *I expect my partner to do what I want done*.

Because stability is so important, each partner expects the other to stay the same. There's a theory about this (origin unknown): *Men expect women not to change, women expect men to change, and they will both be disappointed*. We don't necessarily believe this, but it's something to think about.

One way to keep stability is to be careful about what is said, so communication is often guarded. These people keep a lot of their thoughts and feelings to themselves or revert to telling *little white lies* because the full truth and nothing but the truth might rock the boat. A rocking boat in a conventional relationship is not usually a good thing.

> In the early stages of their relationship Jerry and Susan went out of their way to spend time together. They were affectionate and talked about everything. Now, years later, Jerry gets home from work before Susan and sits at the kitchen table with the newspaper. When Susan gets home and says, *hi*, Jerry doesn't even look up. They do not touch, kiss, or even smile. Susan gets a drink, pets the dog and gets lost in her computer. This is the way it is and this is the way it will stay unless someone gets sick of it and both decide to fix it.

There are lots of relationships like this. You probably know of some. When people are locked into the idea of stability they are often reluctant to acknowledge the signs of change. Jerry and Susan, like so many others, started out with the best intentions. But without continued dedication, attention and excellent communication and problem-solving skills, their relationship will almost certainly crumble with the passing of time.

How about you? Did you used to talk with your partner for hours about everything? Was nothing more important than each other's happiness? Did you get lost in the details of your lives and ignore some of the little things that bothered you?

In conventional relationships, partners often make assumptions such as these:

I know what you're thinking and feeling, though I didn't ask.

You should know what I'm thinking and feeling, even though I didn't tell you.

I know what's best for you but I don't think you know what's best for me.

I've changed my mind about a lot of things but haven't told you about them.

I don't want to know if you've changed.

These assumptions sometimes create irritations that eventually become problems. What do the partners do about them? Nag, sulk, whine, blame or withdraw? Or do they try to fix what's wrong?

As time passes, people in conventional relationships will probably end up one of three ways:

- committed, mostly satisfied, long-term partners

- estranged roommates

- divorced or separated

A committed, comfortable, long-term relationship is rare, but it is possible. Smart people see what's happening when the relationship shows the first signs of trouble and they decide to make things better.

High-Trust: A Plan for Intimacy

Are you happy with your relationship or do you want something better? Do you want to fix what isn't working? The High-Trust Relationship is for people who want excitement, honesty, intimacy and commitment and are willing to undertake a great big challenge!

"Trust" in High-Trust Relationships has three components. The first is the confidence that both people will tell the truth to each other.

The second is that they will keep their agreements. *I believe my partner will do what she or he has agreed to do and will renegotiate when agreements no longer work.*

The third component of trust is the mutual confidence that each is willing and able to deal well with changes, problems, discomfort and crises: *I know my partner is strong and can handle the situations that confront us. My partner is emotionally healthy and does not need to be protected from difficult situations or feelings.*

People who are good candidates for High-Trust Relationships share some common characteristics. They are…

Aware	Honest	Respectful
Independent	Responsible	Compassionate
Tolerant	Committed	Adaptable
Creative	Assertive	Communicative
Affectionate	Generous	Mature

…and they probably have a good sense of humor.

Add other characteristics here:

Let's take a more careful look at these characteristics.

Aware. They are introspective, so they can identify and describe their ideas and feelings clearly. They pay attention to their surroundings and each other.

Honest. They are open, sincere and direct. They don't keep secrets from each other. They talk about the situations that affect them individually and jointly.

Respectful. They admire and appreciate each other. They are polite and complimentary. They don't use sarcasm, put-downs, name-calling, hostile humor, intimidation, force, threat or manipulation.

Independent. They are self-sufficient. They are in a relationship because they want to be, not because they think they have to be. They can take care of themselves.

Responsible. They are in charge of their emotions and actions and ultimately, their own happiness. They keep agreements without being reminded.

Compassionate. They care deeply about each other's needs, emotions and situations. They are empathetic and helpful. Anything given is given with love, not resentment. Some people call this doing something with a *pure heart*.

Tolerant. They accept each other's imperfections. They don't see differences as conflicts and they work to be sure neither person's needs are met at the expense of the other. They are willing to compromise.

Committed. They make the relationship a top priority and are dedicated to helping it thrive. They are involved with each other on every level. They are loyal and bring out the best in each other.

Adaptable. They are not rigid in their habits or thinking. They are comfortable in a wide variety of situations and adjust to changes and surprises.

Remember when we agreed to spend every Thanksgiving with your parents?

Sure, what's up?

Well, the last couple times we've all been together there's been a lot of drinking and arguing. It's just not my idea of a good time, and when we tried to talk to them about it, everybody just shrugged it off and said we were too uptight.

You're right. They didn't even pretend to take us seriously.

No, so I'd like to find a better way to spend the Holiday.

Sounds good to me but we're going to get a lot of grief about it.

That's for sure, but as long as you feel the same way we can come up with something better. How about taking more time tonight to figure out a plan?

Creative: Some of their decisions might seem odd to others. They confront old beliefs and consider new ones, replace old habits with better ones, learn new skills and use them. They make the rules for their own relationship.

Assertive: They are neither aggressive nor passive. They take care of difficulties and irritations early, before they become problems. They don't see themselves as victims, and they don't act out of guilt, anger or fear.

Communicative. They initiate conversations and are good listeners. They take part in discussions and are willing to give their opinions and share important information with each other.

Affectionate. They are attracted to each other and show it.

Generous. They share their time, attention and resources freely.

Mature. They use their own experience, and that of others, for effective decision-making. They are not victims of their upbringing, but assume the responsibilities of adulthood and deal with life's difficulties without hurting themselves or others.

Good Sense of Humor. They can laugh at themselves and they recognize and enjoy the ironies and ambiguities of life. Their humor is never hostile.

These characteristics make it possible for the people in High-Trust Relationships to rely on the strength and integrity of each other. Their actions are consistent with their highest values. Even though these couples are eager to negotiate, they will not sacrifice their most deeply held values for the sake of the relationship. We're not talking here about which way the toilet paper falls or the car is washed, but important concerns such as work ethic, finances, education, cleanliness, child rearing, monogamy, relatives, leisure and other critical issues.

This description of High-Trust Relationships helps you identify some of the specific characteristics so you can enjoy a richer and more intimate bond with your partner. If you don't have a partner, you can use this information to figure out what kind of partner and relationship you're looking for.

You and Chapter 2

What kind of relationship do you have?

If any of the bulleted items about toxic relationships on pages 22 through 24 are true of you, describe what you will do to change them.

Review the description of a conventional relationship on pages 24 through 27. Which of the characteristics do you want to keep and which, if any, do you want to change?

Review the characteristics of people who are good candidates for a High-Trust Relationship on pages 27 through 31, then make notes about what you will do to improve each one. Be sure to state a specific action, not a feeling or attitude.

Example: *I will be more respectful by using "please" and "thank you" more often, and by not criticizing my partner in front of the children or anyone else.*

I will be more **aware** by

I will be more **honest** by

Love Without Lies

I will be more **respectful** by

I will be more **independent** by

I will be more **reliable** by

I will be more **compassionate** by

I will be more **tolerant** by

I will be more **committed** by

I will be more **creative** by

I will be more **assertive** by

I will **communicate better by**

Marty Richards & Diana Novak

I will be more **affectionate** by

I will be more **generous** by

I will be more **mature** by

I will develop or demonstrate my **sense of humor** by

Another exercise is to ask your partner to improve one or more of the characteristics. For example, *I would like you to be more assertive by telling me directly when you are not happy with something I've done.*

Chapter 3
Honesty

> Honesty is absolutely essential in a High-Trust Relationship. It is telling the truth about your ideas, needs, feelings, assumptions, expectations, beliefs and experiences. Dishonesty is either telling a lie or withholding the truth.

Some people think complete honesty is cruel and hurtful, but it doesn't have to be. It can be thoughtful, caring, kind and respectful. We don't suggest that you go around blurting out everything that comes to mind. Stop a few seconds and think before saying something that might be hard for your partner to hear. Why do you want to say it? What good will it do? Is it helpful?

> The only way to speak the truth is to speak lovingly.
>
> *Henry David Thoreau*

Why Is Honesty So Important?

> DeWayne can tell Sheila anything because she doesn't interrupt or make judgments about what he is saying. He feels safe and doesn't have to hide thoughts, feelings and dreams from her even if they are embarrassing or hard to talk about.
>
> DeWayne also listens to Sheila and asks her to tell him anything and everything, even if it's something he has done that bothers her. They never punish one another for what they say.

Remember the feeling of delight and freedom when you were first in love and you'd talk to each other for hours? You'd explore your emotions, ideas and dreams and each discovery seemed to deepen the love and intimacy.

Can those feelings be rekindled? The experience may not seem as intense as it was in the midst of a first love or infatuation, but if both of you want it, and do what it takes to build it, full honesty can add to the excitement and intimacy in your relationship.

How can this happen? First, you will need to learn more about yourself. If you don't know what you think, feel or want, how can you possibly talk about it? You will also need to learn what your partner thinks, feels or wants. This is the basis of an intimate relationship.

Another benefit of honesty is that you don't have to have a good memory. All those white lies and omissions are hard to keep track of. With honesty, both partners know what is going on and no one is being fooled.

When you are consistently honest, your partner can count on what you say. You give an honest opinion when asked for it. You don't agree to do things that you'll resent later. If you do change your mind, you let your partner know so you can work out another agreement together. This is probably the time to mention that when people first start out on the journey to honesty there will be lots of missteps. It's a work in progress.

> Deena had an opportunity to spend an out-of-town weekend with her girlfriends. Her partner, Norman, said he was all for it. But as it came closer to the time of the trip, Norman became aware of resentment he had about the whole idea. They had agreed months before that they needed more time with each other. Norman had even planned time the previous month for them to go away together when Deena pulled out at the last minute saying she had too much to do to leave town.
>
> The more Norman thought about it, the more upset he got. He considered not mentioning this to Deena but remembered their agreement to keep communications open and up-to-date, so he told her how he felt. At first, she was surprised and almost reverted to her old pattern of, *well, you agreed before and it's not fair to bring this up now.* But she resisted the urge and they continued to talk.
>
> After Norman was sure Deena had heard and understood him, he said, *I'm not asking you to cancel your trip and I'm not trying to run a guilt trip on you like I used to. I just wanted you to know what's up with me and it took me awhile to realize what I was feeling.* Deena hugged him and told him how happy she was that he was willing to talk about this. She understood that first feelings are not always final feelings. They congratulated each other about having found a new and better way to talk with each other. They even laughed when they remembered how this kind of situation used to turn into arguments, accusations and their old no-touch, back-to-back sleeping position.

Some couples have conversations like this:

Don:	*Where do you want to go for dinner?*
Maria:	*Anywhere is fine. You decide.*
Don:	*Okay, let's go Italian.*
Maria:	*Oh no. You know I don't like Italian food!*
Don:	*I thought you didn't care.*
Maria:	*And I thought you should have known!*

A better way:

> Don: *Where do you want to go for dinner?*
>
> Maria: *I don't care too much. Anywhere but Italian is fine.*
>
> Don: *Then let's go for sushi, okay?*
>
> Maria: *Sounds good to me.*

Decision-making is quicker and easier when partners are honest and direct. How many times have you thought, *I don't know what my partner wants from me. I'm not a mind-reader.* When you agree to be honest, you don't have to hint, skirt around the truth or test the waters. There is no guesswork, no misunderstanding, no resentment, no martyrs.

> **Honesty is such a lonely word,**
> **Everyone is so untrue.**
> **Honesty is hardly ever heard,**
> **And mostly what I need from you.**
>
> *Billy Joel*

Why Is It So Difficult?

Let the psychologists and philosophers work with this question, but plain and simple: Honesty is not always rewarded. In fact, it is often punished. From the time we were babies, we tried all sorts of ways to get attention. We did what we could to let others know what we felt and what we wanted. We experimented with ways to make ourselves understood.

I don't want to go to grandpa's.

Of course you do – he's your grandpa and you love him.

Or, *Don't be silly. You haven't seen him for a long time.*

Or, *You're being a baby about this. Wipe your tears and get ready.*

Such responses teach the child that his opinions and feelings are not accurate, acceptable or important. The most significant people in his world, his parents, tell him that he's wrong for saying what he wants, and bad for even thinking such things. He is punished for being honest and expressing himself. He may have felt nervous, scared, tired or any of a dozen other emotions. His parents will never know because they missed the chance to find out what he really meant.

We won't be surprised to hear him, as a teen-ager, say, *I dunno, nothin'* or *whatever* when questioned. Even if he knows what he wants, he probably won't talk about it. He learned to hide his feelings and measure his words carefully so he wouldn't be criticized or punished, and he might carry the habit of withholding for the rest of his life. Unless something drastic changes he will suffer the consequences of poor communications and troubled relationships. (And we wonder why so many people are reluctant to communicate honestly.)

It's important to note that there is a big difference between feelings and actions. The boy can complain about the trip to Grandpa's, but still be required to go. It's hard for some parents to let their children express anger and feelings they label as *bad*. When you let your daughter say, *I can't stand my brother,* it doesn't mean you let her say bad words, hit him, or break his toys. Ideas and emotions need to be acknowledged. That's how people learn about themselves and others. Bad behavior should be prevented or controlled, but ideas and emotions should be accepted. That is how people learn to be honest with themselves and others.

Be Careful What You Ask For.

There's no doubt about it—honesty is not for the faint-hearted. When people listen to each other they won't always like what they hear. They might even be frustrated, hurt or disappointed and those feelings have to be dealt with. Some people won't get the intimacy they hoped for, and some revelations may uncover intolerable weaknesses, compromised values or unacceptable behavior. Respect and even love might be lost. The whole relationship might suffer.

For some people a high level of honesty causes too much discomfort and they would rather lead a more guarded or comfortable life. But over time, if they learn to be open with each other without too many bad results, honesty becomes an important and exciting part of the relationship.

When you learn to recognize and talk about your feelings and have an agreement to be honest with each other, the ideal is that you build an atmosphere of trust with your partner. Unfortunately, while honesty is an important step toward intimacy, it doesn't guarantee it. A couple needs to decide whether honesty is worth the risks.

What About Secrets?

Partners should decide together which, if any, subjects will be off limits. If these avoided subjects have no impact on the relationship, leaving them alone will probably not cause problems. Here are some examples of topics that might be considered off limits once they have been fully discussed.

- differences in deeply held values

- previous marriages/relationships

- problems of the past such as addictions, illegal activities, or abusive or violent behavior

- serious medical or psychological issues

However, all serious past issues must be revealed before a couple enters into a committed relationship. As with any decision, each partner should bring up an off limits topic if it is affecting the relationship in any way and at any time. It's only fair.

Do you like to have your own thoughts, dreams, and fantasies without sharing them with your partner? Or are you an open book? What number would you give yourself?

```
Privacy_____Openness
   1     2     3     4     5     6     7     8     9     10
```

See where you are on this scale. Where do you think your partner is on the scale? There is no right or wrong. The important point is that partners talk about their privacy needs with each other. Of course, if one partner expects the other to share every thought or feeling, and the other wants more privacy, communication might be difficult. They need to explore the difference, then find a middle ground where each both can be comfortable.

Taylor:	*You seem very quiet and withdrawn lately. What's going on?*
Sam:	*Nothing, I'm fine.*
Taylor:	*Well, you're more quiet than usual. Is there something we need to talk about?*
Sam:	*It doesn't have anything to do with you and I said I don't want to talk about it.*

> Taylor: *Well, okay, but I sure feel left out when you keep things to yourself.*

Privacy limits intimacy. The more you trust each other, the more thoughts and feelings you will reveal. The more your partner listens with respect, the more you share. That is how intimacy is built.

Warning! It's important to limit or refuse telling your deep feelings, ideas and dreams to people who do not treat you with respect. If you know from previous experience that your partner, or anyone else for that matter, does not accept or respect such revelations, don't subject yourself to their disapproval or condemnation. What's the point?

> Carla was brought up to avoid talking about religion, sex, money or politics because of the discord that usually resulted. She applied this belief to all of her relationships, including with Rick, with whom she was falling in love.
>
> Rick came from a family that talked freely about nearly everything. Even though the discussions were sometimes heated or even disturbing, family members knew they could air their differences, explore "sensitive" issues, and reveal their most personal trials and triumphs. Rick knew he had to have this kind of honesty with his own partner.
>
> Carla was shocked at how revealing Rick was, and Rick was surprised at how tentative and deceptive Carla's conversation was about so many topics that Rick thought were important.
>
> Rick talked with Carla about this difference (of course he did). He let her know that the issue of openness was a "must have" in their relationship. It took time but Carla discovered that she could say anything to Rick without fear of being rejected or punished. She knew he might be hurt or angry but also knew he could handle the discomfort without taking it out on her. This atmosphere of honesty was difficult at first but eventually gave her a sense of freedom and intimacy she had never experienced. Their relationship improved with every discussion and revelation.

When you choose people with whom you will be more open,

you will build relationships in which you can reveal more about yourself and set the scene for others to be more honest with you. Here are some kinds of dishonesty:

<table>
<tr><td>Statement:
Blatant Lie:</td><td>Where were you?
I was working late. (She was at a bar with friends.)</td></tr>
<tr><td>Statement:
Withholding:</td><td>Did you go shopping today?
I just picked up a few things. (He spent $400 on video games.)</td></tr>
<tr><td>Statement:
Misleading
or Diverting</td><td>Do you like my new outfit?
We just got gas last Friday and I noticed it's almost on empty.</td></tr>
<tr><td>Statement:

Sarcasm:</td><td>Would you mind watching the kids while I do some work?
Oh sure, that's my favorite way to spend time after working all day!</td></tr>
<tr><td>Statement
Hinting</td><td>What do you think about Bob's new look?
He looks great because he shaves every day. (She hates her partner's beard.)</td></tr>
<tr><td>Statement
Minimizing:</td><td>Does it bother you when I call Sharon?
No, I know you have to talk with your ex-wife sometimes. (She hates any contact between the two of them.)</td></tr>
<tr><td>Statement
Exaggerating:</td><td>Are you angry about something?
Of course I am. You're always late. (She was late twice last week.)</td></tr>
</table>

Why Are People Dishonest?

There are lots of reasons people are dishonest. Here are some of them:

- They don't know how to talk about their feelings, needs, ideas and values.

- They are ashamed or embarrassed about something they have done.

- They think their partner is too emotional, weak, defensive or insecure to accept the truth.

- They are afraid their partner will be angry, judgmental, disappointed, or might hurt or punish them.

- They worry that their partner may not keep the information private.

- They think their partner may blow the information out of proportion, minimize or ignore it.

- They are dependent on their partner and don't want to risk losing the relationship.

These justifications might make sense at the time because they help avoid the discomfort of dealing with difficult situations. But don't fool yourself—they are not harmless. In the long run, avoiding the real problem gets in the way of intimacy. Admit the fear, work through it and take the risks that go with honesty if you want a High-Trust Relationship.

Imagine yourself in a situation where you have deceived your partner. Sometimes a *little white lie* seems like the easiest way out of a difficult problem, so you do it, perhaps telling yourself that it is for your partner's own good. The pattern snowballs until each lie has to be followed by another. This goes on until you are stressed out, anxious and feeling guilty. Even if you are *lucky* and your partner doesn't find out, you still may have damaged the relationship. When good people break promises or compromise their values, they may be ashamed or guilty, and pull away, blame their partner, or damage the relationship in other ways.

What happens when you get caught? Your partner's trust in you is damaged. Once that happens it is difficult or impossible to regain it. Even when you say you're sorry and promise never to lie again, it may not be enough for your partner. If you show that you have changed, your partner may forgive but will never forget. If a similar situation comes up, the doubts will be there.

> Doug's wife, Allie, was out of town, supposedly visiting her sister, when he discovered their credit card was maxed out and the payment overdue. He was shocked since she took care of the finances and always assured him that she kept payments up-to-date. He phoned his wife's sister only to find out that she hadn't even talked to Allie for weeks, so both of them were puzzled and worried. When Allie returned the next day Doug was relieved, then furious, as the story unravelled. Doug discovered a string of lies and the couple was now in crisis. It took years to straighten out their finances and Doug simply couldn't trust his wife anymore. The deception caused anger, guilt and loss of respect. The damage couldn't be repaired and the marriage couldn't be saved.

Another kind of dishonesty is holding back information or telling half-truths. By doing this, you decide for your partner what information is okay to share and what is not. When you *protect* the other from the whole truth, it shows a lack of trust in your partner's ability to cope with it. It says, *I am stronger/smarter/more capable than you* or, *I know what is best for you and the relationship.*

A harmful effect of avoiding the whole truth is that your partner doesn't get the benefit of what she or he needs to know to make good choices and to be equal in the relationship.

Withholding is selfish. So, rather than *protecting* your partner, you are just protecting yourself. The truth is you just don't want to face the unpleasant music.

> Susan and Kim have been together for several years and agreed to be sexually exclusive. When she was on a business trip, Susan had a brief affair with a co-worker. She felt guilty afterwards and wanted to tell Kim about it, but Susan took the easy way out, and decided it would only stir up more trouble. After months of fretting, Susan thought about their promise to be faithful and honest, and decided to tell Kim the truth. Kim was hurt and angry, but also appreciated Susan's honesty. At least now, Kim had all the information needed to make a decision about what to do.

Let's talk about the worst-case scenario of possible reactions to dishonesty such as, *You did it; now it's my turn.* Or, *I'll make you pay for it!* You can use your imagination, remember times in your own life, or watch television and movies to find how dishonesty ruins relationships and the people in them.

Wrapping It Up.

- When partners accept the truth about each other, any emotion, idea or dream can be shared. This helps the relationship stay fresh and interesting.

- There's no doubt about it; honesty is difficult. If you were taught to keep quiet about your ideas or emotions, it might be pretty hard to talk about them now. It will take work and patience.

- Couples may decide not to talk about certain subjects because they know they will never agree.

- Of course you can keep your private thoughts, dreams, feelings and other secrets to yourself, but it will interfere with the depth of intimacy.

- Dishonesty shows a lack of respect for your partner and kills trust. In short, dishonesty destroys relationships.

> **Honesty is the foundation of a High-Trust Relationship**

You and Chapter 3

How Honest Are You?

Think of something about yourself that you have not told your partner. It could be a past action, a private dream or fantasy, a problem, or a personal value. What is it and why haven't you talked about it?

Let's look at your experience with dishonesty. Think back over your life and identify a situation where you told a lie. Why did you do it? Were there any complications or problems caused because of it? How did the situation get resolved? If you were faced with that situation now, how would you act?

Chapter 4
Communication – The Key to Intimacy

Both partners in a High-Trust Relationship must use excellent communication skills to make it work. The basic skills are:

1. Know yourself

2. Speak clearly

3. Listen carefully

The first step of clear communication is self-awareness—how well you know yourself. You can only be as honest with your partner as you are with yourself. As you work to figure out what makes you tick you'll have to acknowledge your faults and foibles, weaknesses and strengths, then find the words to describe how you feel and what you think.

You might be surprised, or even embarrassed, when you look at the unflattering truth. Surprisingly, even praise and compliments make some people uncomfortable if they don't see themselves as others do. When you hear things you don't like, you may think *I don't do that!* Or, *That's not true*! That kind of reaction is called defensiveness. Defensiveness prevents people from learning about themselves or others.

So, you can protect yourself from things you don't want to hear and learn nothing, or you can listen to, think about, and maybe even change your mind for the better. This will be difficult at times but there is a lot to gain from it. We'll show you how to start the process.

How To Learn More About Yourself

- Pay attention to yourself. What do you feel, think, want, expect?

- Accept your emotions just as they are. Choose your actions.

- Notice when and how you are defensive. What are you are protecting yourself from? Replace defensiveness with an eagerness to learn.

- Listen to compliments, criticism and complaints and learn from them.

- Take classes, read books, talk with trusted friends and family to learn more about yourself.

- When you learn something new about yourself, talk with your partner about it. That's one way to improve communication and build intimacy.

- Learn a lot of words that describe your emotions, and see how accurate you can be when thinking or talking about them. We've listed some here.

thrilled	unhappy	loveable	pleased
sorrowful	mean	mad	loving
melancholy	trapped	crabby	joyous
remorseful	threatened	annoyed	disturbed
ecstatic	miserable	terrible	acrimonious
excited	distraught	tense	spiteful
confident	blue	terrified	jealous
grateful	worried	afraid	pressured
disgruntled	defeated	scared	obnoxious
happy	bitchy	impressed	lonely
flustered	shocked	infuriated	ornery
delighted	grateful	glad	silly

The more accurately you identify and express your emotions, the more you will find out about yourself and the better your communications will be. The words *pissed* or *angry* just cover up the real emotions behind them. Work to find more descriptive words for your deeper and more real emotions. The same is true for "positive" emotions. If *I love you* is the only way you express affection verbally, occasionally replace it with, *I appreciate you for*…or, *I admire how you*…or, *I respect you for*…

You and your partner will learn a lot from using words that describe your emotions more accurately.

How To Talk About Yourself

Now we talk about you, the sender of a message; the one who starts the conversation, gives information or wants change.

First, before you even open your mouth to talk about something important, prepare yourself. You don't have to blurt out every emotion or thought that goes through your head. Just be clear and concise. Your partner may be surprised, even shocked, when you change how you talk, but if you have a loving relationship, the good results will soon be obvious.

- Don't expect your partner to read your mind. It doesn't work.

- Ask yourself, *What is my goal; what am I trying to do?*

- *What words and tone will help my partner understand me?*

- Think about the setting. *Is this the right time and place to talk?*

- Limit yourself to one issue at a time.

- Talk about the present or recent past. There's no point in bringing up old issues unless they are still causing problems.

- Keep your message short and to the point so your partner can absorb what you say.

- Keep your voice and tone respectful.

- Don't blame your partner for what you do or how you feel.

- Don't try to change how your partner feels or thinks.

- When you want your partner to do something, ask for it. Be specific and direct.

- Don't hint, withdraw, call names, threaten, sulk or use sarcasm. It's not nice and it makes things worse.

How To Say What You Mean

Here are some ways to get your message across when you are the sender and want to be clear and direct.

State the Cold, Hard Facts (Objective Statement): This is a fact, described without any assumptions, judgments, preferences, emotions or opinions. *The party starts at 8 tonight.*

Talk About Yourself (Self-Disclosure or Subjective Information): This is how you report your feelings, assumptions, ideas, preferences or opinions. *I'm worried about arriving late.*

Ask For a Change (Request): This is a brief, direct, specific way to say exactly what you want done. *Will you please be ready to leave by 7:30?*

Let It Be (Natural Consequence): This is what will naturally happen if the situation is left alone. *If we get to the party late, all the good food will be gone.*

I'll Do It My Way (Independent Action): This is what you will do on your own. *I'm leaving for the party at 7:30.*

Don't use all the options at once or in every case. Just pick and choose the ones that help you express yourself clearly. At first, they will seem awkward but with practice you'll find that they even help you think more clearly. Here are some examples of how they can be combined to send a clear message.

I see that checks #870 and #871 are not recorded in the checkbook. (objective statement) + *I'm frustrated about this problem.* (self-disclosure) + *Will you please write it down every time you make out a check?* (request)

Or, *If we get to the party late, all the good food will be gone.* (objective statement) + *I'm hungry.* (self-disclosure) + *so I'll leave here at 7:30.* (independent action) + *I'd sure like you to go with me.* (self-disclosure)

Or, *You didn't pick me up after work today until 5:30.* (objective statement) + *In the future, please call my cell phone if you're not going to be on time.* (request) + *That will leave me some options.* (self-disclosure)

Question: Will clear sending always work?

Answer: It increases the chance that your partner will understand what you mean, but it won't guarantee that your partner will respond the way you want. Your partner will decide what to do with what you say.

Success depends on...

- how clear your message is,

- how your partner interprets the message,

- your partner's willingness to understand,

- what your partner wants,

- how good your partner's skills are,

- how good the relationship is.

A caring partner wants to understand what you are saying. If your partner doesn't seem interested in your ideas or feelings and isn't willing to listen to you, there's a bigger problem than communication. You need to find out what that problem is. While your independent changes can influence your partner, it takes two willing people to have the quality of communication that a High-Trust Relationship requires.

Note: The sender is the one who starts the conversation, usually because he or she wants to give information or wants a change.

> **The purpose of clear sending is to increase the chances that your partner understands you.**

How To Listen With Love:

- The listener is the one being talked to and who wants to understand what the sender is saying.

- Careful listening is absolutely essential for an intimate relationship to thrive.

Now you will learn how to listen so your partner is more likely to be honest with you.

> Roger got home after work as usual but Jill wasn't there. He found a letter on the kitchen table. *I've had enough and I've left you. You're a good guy and our first ten years were wonderful, but these last few years have been awful for me. When I tried to talk with you about it and asked you to go to counseling, you ignored me so often that I gave up trying. Now I feel free to leave and make a life of my own. I am so sad that we let our love die. I will always have a special place in my heart for you. Good luck.*

Roger couldn't believe it. He thought she had just been in a bad mood for a long time and he was waiting for her to feel better. When Jill came by a few days later to pack up her things, he begged her to go to counseling. But it was too late. She didn't love him anymore and was already enjoying a new sense of relief and freedom. Their friends and family were shocked. Roger and Jill always seemed so happy. Jill had done a good job of hiding her unhappiness from all of them.

Imagine what might have happened if Roger had taken Jill seriously and listened carefully when she first tried to talk about her unhappiness. What if he took her in his arms at the first mention of a problem and promised her he'd do anything to help? What if he would have been enthusiastic about fixing what was wrong? What if he made their relationship a top priority? What if he would have taken the initiative to make an appointment with a counselor? We'll never know. Neither will he.

People usually give lots of clues before they decide to do something drastic. But unless the partner cares, listens and wants to learn and solve problems, the result is often a sad one.

In a High-Trust Relationship every thought, feeling, opinion, hurt, disappointment, dream or joy can be discussed without fear of judgment, rejection or ridicule. That is how intimacy is built. Both partners know they need to listen and accept what is being said so they can learn from it. All ideas and emotions should be treated as important, even if they are hard to talk about and harder to hear.

Careful listening means that you let your partner know you heard what was said, whether or not you agree. As the listener, it's not your job to talk about your own opinions or reactions, but to listen and understand your partner's point of view. Then the two of you can discuss the situation. This will take good deal of self-control at first when you are learning the skill, but in most cases, it will be worth it.

> The purpose of good listening is to understand what your partner knows, believes, thinks, feels, wants or expects.

Benefits Of Good Listening

- You will teach your partner that honesty is rewarded, rather than punished.

- You will know about potential problems before they became crises. Good listening prevents bad surprises.

- You will have less stress as you consider your partner's opinions, rather than arguing or getting hurt or angry.

- You will show respect for your partner.

- You will learn about your partner and increase intimacy.

I'm Not Defensive. I'm Not, I'm Not, I'm Not!

Defensive listening is the opposite of careful listening.

Marty Richards & Diana Novak

Defensiveness is anything you do or say that gets in the way of understanding exactly what your partner says and means. You'll be a much better listener if you recognize your defensive reactions and replace them with more respectful and effective ones.

Defensive phrases, such as the ones that follow, make clear, honest exchanges almost impossible.

Yeah, yeah I know that already.

I like doing it this way.

You're wrong.

What's wrong with you?

Whatever.

I'm busy.

I don't want to talk about it.

That's a silly way to feel.

You'll feel better tomorrow.

You can't possibly believe that!

You're taking all this too hard.

You're not so perfect yourself.

You don't think I understand, but I do.

Thank you for sharing.

Oh no, here we go again.

Defensiveness shows a lack of respect for your partner and interferes with intimacy. It keeps you from learning important information about your partner and yourself. To be blunt, it keeps you ignorant about a lot of important things.

> **When you stop being defensive you will learn what your partner wants you to know.**

The four basic skills below will help you be a better listener:

<u>Passive Listening:</u> Pay attention and don't interrupt. This shows you are willing to understand what your partner is saying.

<u>Paraphrasing:</u> Repeat in your own words what you heard. This shows your partner whether or not you understand the message.

<u>Active Listening:</u> Paraphrase and acknowledge the emotion expressed by your partner. This shows you understand your partner's message <u>and</u> feelings.

<u>Quality Questions:</u> After you've listened awhile, you can ask some questions to get more information. Be careful not to take the focus away from your partner's message.

Quality questions are*: When? What? Who? Which? Where?* and *How?* The question *Why?* sometimes gets in the way of good conversation. It often elicits, *I don't know* or, *because* as a response. *Why?* sometimes triggers defensiveness because it is often interpreted as being an accusation. (If a couple has excellent communication skills, the question *why?* probably won't interfere with the discussion. It will simply be seen as an effort to get more information.)

After you listen carefully to your partner, it's a good time to offer your interest and support:

- Is there anything else you want me to know?

- Is there some way I can help?

- What do you need now?

- I've got some ideas. Do you want to hear them?

When you first practice listening like this, it may seem phony, both to you and your partner, but like any other skill it gets more comfortable with practice.

Listening Guidelines: If you want to learn new ways to listen so your partner is more likely to be honest with you, consider these suggestions:

- Remember that the goal of listening is to learn.

- Tell your partner you are interested and want to understand.

- Let your partner set the pace of the conversation and decide what to say. Give your full attention and don't interrupt.

- Paraphrase and use questions to be sure you understand what your partner wants you to know.

- Acknowledge not only the words your partner says, but also the emotion behind it.

- Avoid guessing or trying to read your partner's mind.

- Don't say or do anything that is likely to make your partner reluctant to talk to you, even if you don't particularly like what you hear. Be honest and say something like, *This is hard for me to hear but I'll do my best.*

- Thank your partner for being honest with you.

Criticism, Complaints and Compliments

For most people, complaints and criticism are pretty hard to take. It is difficult to hear that someone thinks you are imperfect. What a shock! But one of the most useful skills is non-defensive listening. Instead of being offended by criticism, complaints or opinions, consider them as opportunities to learn. When you start doing this, good things will happen.

- You will have less stress. It takes a lot of energy to argue or defend yourself.

- You will get information that will help you improve yourself.

- You will defuse highly charged confrontations.

- You will discover potential problem situations before they become crises.

- You will give your partner an opportunity to explore his or her ideas and feelings.

- You will demonstrate self-control and maturity.

- You will provide a good example for others.

The next section will help you identify your usual defensive reactions then replace them with more helpful responses.

When you hear something you don't like or don't agree with, which defenses do you use? Circle them.

show anger	gossip	leave
ignore	act macho	play dumb
use guilt	worry	nag
show resentment	whine	laugh
use logic only	make excuses	shop
get dramatic	talk a lot	stop talking
get busy	act weak	act tough
change the subject	play the victim	argue
get hurt	blame	get drunk
pretend not to care	use sarcasm	sulk
act superior	use humor	cry

There are more. Add any others you can think of.

Defensive reactions get in the way of empathizing with and understanding your partner, or anyone else for that matter.

Here are some guidelines for listening to criticism and complaints. They will also help you listen to ideas you don't agree with when you want to learn and keep communication open. Non-defensive listening is a characteristic of confident and empathetic people.

1. **Remember** that criticism is someone else's opinion, feelings, or an attempt to influence you. Criticism doesn't mean that you need to be manipulated, intimidated, angry or defensive.

2. **Take a deep breath**. Your job as a good listener is to learn.

   I want to understand. This is important to me.
   Please tell me about it.
   Let's talk. Is this a good time?

3. **Acknowledge** the importance of your partner's message.

   I'm glad you brought this up. I thought you were upset about something.

   I can see this is important to you. I'm ready to listen.

4. **Agree** with any part of the complaint or criticism you can. (This takes the discussion to a different and better level.)

   You're right. I did do that. Or, *Yes, sometimes I do that.*

   I know that bothers you a lot. It was a big mistake on my part.

   That was thoughtless of me. I'm sorry.

5. **Use quality questions** to be sure you understand your partner, and before you answer a criticism or complaint.

When did I do that?

What bothers you about what I did?

Will you give me an example of what I did?

What would you like me to do instead?

6. **Agree to change** or admit that you won't, then offer to help solve the problem.

   I'm working on that. Will you remind me if I forget?

   I know that bothers you. Let's keep talking about it until we find a good compromise.

   To be honest, I probably won't change this, but let's see if we can work something out so it doesn't bother you so much.

7. **Thank your partner for being honest.**

   I'm glad you brought this up...I like to know what's on your mind.

> **The purpose of listening to criticism and complaints is to understand what your partner knows, believes, values, thinks, feels, wants or expects.**

Note: Sometimes you just won't want to learn more. These skills will even help in those situations. If someone says something like, *I'm disappointed in you. You could do better than that!* Take a deep breath and say something like, *Yes, I probably could.* Or, your critical mom who usually pushes your buttons, looks around your house and says, *What a mess! Didn't I teach you better than this?* Simply smile and say, *Yes, you did.* You don't have to explain anything or try to change her mind. End of conversation and end of manipulation. We're not pretending this kind of reply enhances intimacy. It doesn't. But we aren't talking about intimacy in these cases. Your non-defensive reactions will simply change the course of the conversation and help break your usual habits.

As strange as it may seem, some people are even defensive about compliments. They might think that a compliment is insincere or manipulative. They may not want to hear it because they don't agree with it. Here are ways that some people reject compliments:

- *You're just trying to get something.*

- *You're just saying that.*

- *You don't mean that.*

- *What do you want anyway?*

- *Oh, I am not!*

- *I should have done it higher/faster/better/sooner.*

- *Why are you saying that?*

Do you ever deny compliments? Well, stop it. Accept them all. You might start enjoying, and maybe even believing them. Wouldn't *that* be nice?

So, what to do instead? Easy. Say, *Thank you,* and remember that you were just given important information. Instead of trying to prove how wrong the compliment might be, think about what part of the compliment might be true of you. You don't have to agree with it, just accept it for what it is—someone's opinion or an attempt to get you to do something. In a High-Trust Relationship, any compliment from your partner will be a sincere one.

Remember that people have different opinions about the same thing. The objective truth is not always important when you listen to criticism, complaints and compliments.

Question: But what if someone is trying to manipulate me with compliments?

Answer: Don't fall for it! Don't argue, accuse or deny the compliment. Treat it as though it's sincere, then decide what, if anything, to do about it.

Karen: *Honey, your lasagna is so much better than mine.*

Dave: *Thank you.*

Karen: *So you'll make it tonight?*

Dave: *No, but I'll be glad to do the dishes.*

Now, isn't that easy? Well, maybe not, especially at first. But once you realize that criticism, complaints and compliments are simply another person's opinions, feelings or requests, you'll be able to remain a listener, at least at first. Then, when you've understood to your partner's satisfaction, you can discuss the subject or suggest solving a problem if there is one.

> **You know you listened well when the sender is satisfied that you understood the message exactly as he or she intended it to be heard.**

We mentioned earlier that these communication skills will probably improve any relationship. Imagine how your life will improve when you understand yourself better so you can send clearer messages and listen non-defensively. You will be a better friend, lover, thinker, student, teacher, salesperson, executive, consultant or parent.

Once you are familiar with the basic sending and listening skills, you can use them to help you solve problems. That's what the next chapter is about.

You and Chapter 4

Increase Self Awareness

Review pages 49-52 and choose two of the suggested items that will increase your self-awareness. Plan to use them in the next few weeks, then choose a couple more and practice them. Do the same with the others.

What are your first two?

Practice Sending A Clear Message

What is something your partner does that you'd like changed but you've not discussed because of its sensitive nature or your fear of the reaction you would get?

Now review the suggestions on pages 52-54 and write the message using clear, non-judgmental language. Be as clear and specific as possible so your partner will know exactly what you mean.

When your message is in its best form, let your partner know that you have something important to discuss and you'd like to take some time to talk about it.

Practice Careful Listening

Think of something your partner told you that you didn't like hearing so you responded defensively. Refer to the list on page 62 to help identify and label your feelings.

What did you say or do?

Look through the suggestions for careful listening on pages 63 and 64, then decide which of them (or which combination) you think might have been best for you to use in the situation above.

A good way to practice this is to go back to your partner and ask to have this conversation again, this time with your new responses. See how it goes. Use this same exercise to learn new ways to respond to criticism or hard-to-hear compliments.

If you want to improve your skills, here's a self-assessment for you and one for your partner.

Marty Richards & Diana Novak

My Self Assessment

Decide how well these statements characterize your typical behavior.

5 = almost always true   4 = usually true   3 = true about half the time

2 = occasionally true   1 = rarely true

___ 1. I know and use a wide variety of words to describe my emotions.
___ 2. I acknowledge my feelings, but think before I act.
___ 3. I consider the possible consequences of my words, actions and decisions.
___ 4. When I'm bothered by what my partner does, I describe the problem behavior and its consequences without hinting, teasing, name-calling, threatening, sarcasm or blaming.
___ 5. When I know what I want my partner to do, I make direct requests.
___ 6. I avoid guessing or trying to read my partner's mind.
___ 7. I am willing to change my mind when given new information.
___ 8. I assume responsibility for myself, and avoid blaming others for what I do or how I feel.
___ 9. I ask for my partner's support, help, or clarification when I want it.
___10. I recognize my typical defensive reactions and work to minimize them.
___11. I give my full attention when my partner talks with me.
___12. I often paraphrase and use questions to understand my partner.
___13. I listen well to opinions that are different from mine.
___14. After listening to my partner I offer help if it's needed.
___15. I invite criticism and suggestions, and listen to them non-defensively.
___16. I use self-disclosure to tell my partner about my opinions, values, expectations and feelings.
___17. I ask my partner to talk honestly about any complaints or suggestions.
___18. I show my partner appreciation for being honest with me.
___19. I frequently ask my partner to talk to me about things that are important to him/her.
___20. I show that I am interested in my partner's interests.

_____Total Score

Scoring Key:

80-100   Wow. If you've been objective about your assessment you are probably known as an excellent communicator and others find it easy to talk honestly with you.

60-79:   Pretty good. It will help a lot if you work to improve the items you marked "3" or lower.

50-74:   Your relationship is probably in trouble but will improve if you make a major effort to develop your skills.

49 or less: Your relationships are suffering whether you know it or not. You will benefit from some therapy, coaching, counseling or classes.

Love Without Lies

My Partner's Self-Assessment

Decide how well these statements characterize your typical behavior.

5 = almost always true   4 = usually true   3 = true about half the time

2 = occasionally true   1 = rarely true

___ 1. I know and use a wide variety of words to describe my emotions.
___ 2. I acknowledge my feelings, but think before I act.
___ 3. I consider the possible consequences of my words, actions and decisions.
___ 4. When I'm bothered by what my partner does, I describe the problem behavior and its consequences without hinting, teasing, name-calling, threatening, sarcasm or blaming.
___ 5. When I know what I want my partner to do, I make direct requests.
___ 6. I avoid guessing or trying to read my partner's mind.
___ 7. I am willing to change my mind when given new information.
___ 8. I assume responsibility for myself, and avoid blaming others for what I do or how I feel.
___ 9. I ask for my partner's support, help, or clarification when I want it.
___10. I recognize my typical defensive reactions and work to minimize them.
___11. I give my full attention when my partner talks with me.
___12. I often paraphrase and use questions to understand my partner.
___13. I listen well to opinions that are different from mine.
___14. After listening to my partner I offer help if it is needed.
___15. I invite criticism and suggestions, and listen to them non-defensively.
___16. I use self-disclosure to tell my partner about my opinions, values, expectations and feelings.
___17. I ask my partner to talk honestly about any complaints or suggestions.
___18. I show my partner appreciation for being honest with me.
___19. I frequently ask my partner to talk to me about things that are important to him/her.
___20. I show that I am interested in my partner's interests.

_____ Total Score

Scoring Key:

80-100   Wow. If you've been objective about your assessment you are probably known as an excellent communicator and others find it easy to talk honestly with you.

60-79:   Pretty good. It will help a lot if you work to improve the items you marked "3" or lower.

50-74:   Your relationship is probably in trouble but will improve if you make a major effort to develop your skills.

49 or less: Your relationships are suffering whether you know it or not. You will benefit from some therapy, coaching, counseling or classes.

Chapter 5
Problem-Solving

Since when are you the big expert?
You can't possibly want that!
What's wrong with you anyway?
That's the craziest thing I ever heard of.
It's my way or the highway!
I make the money, so I'll decide.
That's just not normal!

Sound familiar? Conflict can be found anywhere and anytime there are two or more people. The very thought of conflict is enough to make some people retreat, argue, sulk, fight or do other things that make matters worse.

Conflict is a struggle or a quarrel; a situation where there is a disagreement of ideas or interests; a disturbance that results from an unwillingness to reconcile differences. Problem-solving is a method for finding solutions.

Conflict: Trouble Or Opportunity?

Imagine what life and love would be like if you could talk about any problem with the assurance that your partner is eager to work until you find a solution that satisfies you both. Too good to be true? It's rare, that's for sure, but many couples do just that. This chapter will help you find new ways to deal with differences and conflict so they are not frightening or damaging to you, your partner and the relationship.

High-Trust Relationships are not common. They require extraordinary skills to maintain them, and problem-solving is one of them. This section suggests some good ways to deal with conflict.

> He insists the toothpaste tube is rolled neatly from the bottom. She squeezes it any old way.
>
> She wants to spend their savings on a major home remodel and he dreams of owning a boat. Years of arguments have only increased the tension between them.
>
> He wants children and she does not.
>
> His ideal weekend is to spend the time immersed in beer and watching sports on t.v. She resents the impact it has on the relationship.
>
> She's happy with having sex once a month or less, and he's only satisfied when they make love at least twice a week.

In any relationship there are differences about values, opinions or preferences. They are not necessarily problems, especially when each person considers alternative opinions and respects individuality in the relationship. Unfortunately, differences are often seen as the basis for arguments and conflict. For example, one person sees a movie and likes it, and the other doesn't. What do most people do? They start trying to talk each other out of their opinions.

> *That was the best movie I've seen in a long time.*
>
> *What, are you kidding? It was awful.*
>
> *Well, what makes you an expert about movies? We hardly ever go anymore.*

If you weren't so cheap, we'd go out more often.

Not likely! I don't want to go to the movies with you again anyway. We always end up arguing about them.

What started out as a simple difference of opinion escalated to an exchange of right vs. wrong, insults and bad feelings on both sides. Instead, conflict could be seen as an opportunity to have a respectful, though spirited, discussion.

That was the best movie I've seen in a long time.

Oh, really? I didn't like it at all.

Well, we've always liked different kinds of movies. You're a good sport and I'm glad you came with me since I've waited a long time to see it. Let's be sure we go to your first choice next time.

You're great. I'll take you up on that and treat you to dinner.

It should be obvious that the first example leaves both people feeling awful. The second is respectful, feels good and there's another date planned. The couple knows how to compromise, and they laugh about their differences.

Problems result when conflicts are met with ineffective *solutions* that ignore the needs of one partner. Such decisions mean that one person exercises power over the other, or one person gives in and resents it. This kind of power ultimately leads to resentment, anger and guilt—no friends of a loving relationship. Differences and conflicts must be acknowledged and treated with respect or they become on-going problems with escalating damage to the relationship. Conflicts provide opportunities to know yourself and your partner better, and they can even add excitement and intimacy if they are met with loving intentions and good skills.

When differences cause conflicts they either damage the relationship, or they are resolved so that both people are satisfied and the relationship becomes richer. The number of differences in a relationship is not particularly important. When they become conflicts, a good measure of the health of that relationship is how the people involved deal with them. In a High-Trust Relationship differences, problems and conflicts are met with the commitment to work toward solutions that address the needs of both partners.

Love Without Lies

The next section explores some common beliefs, emotions and reactions to conflict, invites you to assess how you deal with it, and suggests ways to reach good solutions.

Common Beliefs About Conflict	Beliefs That Help Solve Problems
Fault must be established before a solution is found.	Conflicts can be resolved without establishing fault or blame.
There is only one right solution to most problems.	There are several good solutions to most problems.
Resistance should be met with a more forceful argument.	Resistance should be met by understanding my partner's point of view.
Proving I'm right increases my status with my partner.	Flexibility and empathy are likely to earn my partner's respect.
Conflict indicates a problem in a relationship.	Conflict can contribute to the health and vitality of the relationship.
In conflict, someone is sure to be hurt, angry or disappointed.	Compromise and mutual respect result in satisfaction and increased intimacy.
My partner will take unfair advantage of me if given the opportunity.	My partner is reasonable and generous and wants to find a good solution.

Put a checkmark by the beliefs listed on the previous page that you are most likely to hold when you are in a conflict.

Usual Reactions To Conflict—What People Feel

confused	afraid	angry
disgusted	defensive	hurt
annoyed	tense	anxious
helpless	resentful	guilty

What emotions do you usually feel when you and your partner have a conflict? Use those above or add your own.

Usual Reactions To Conflict—What People Do

Emotions may trigger actions, but they don't cause them. Emotions just happen. People decide what actions to take. Some of those actions are:

cry	leave	sulk
pretend to agree	complain	show anger
change the subject	nag	withdraw
blame	gossip	call names
withhold affection	get sarcastic	argue

deny there's a problem

Have we forgotten any? List them here.

What do you usually do?

Emotionally mature people choose actions that help.

> **Conflict is inevitable, but combat is optional.**
> Max Lucade

Now that we've identified some common beliefs, emotions and actions that often accompany conflicts, we offer some suggestions for resolving the resulting problems.

A Better Way

- Remember that the person who is bothered has the responsibility to initiate problem-solving.

- State the problem or conflict clearly and ask for help to solve it.

- The partner who is listening has the responsibility to help solve the problem. People who love each other want their partner to be satisfied.

- The earlier and better an issue is confronted, the more likely it will be solved without major hurt, anger or resentment. Take care of them when they are just little irritations.

- Set up a time and place for the problem-solving session. Be sure to plan for as much time as you think you will need.

- Give information in short phrases and ask for feedback to be sure your partner understands you.

- Listen non-defensively.

- Don't blame, yell, call names or withdraw.

- Deal with one issue at a time.

- Don't tackle a difficult subject when either of you is overly tired or stressed. If things get overwhelming call off the session temporarily and agree to continue at a specified time.

People who use good problem-solving skills need to be able to say of themselves…

- *I know the difference between my opinions and the objective truth.*

- *I listen with interest to opinions that are different from mine.*

- *When I have a complaint or request, I ask my partner to talk it over with me.*

- *When I don't understand something I ask for clarification.*

- *I am willing to change my point of view when given new information.*

- *I listen to criticism and complaints non-defensively.*

- *I express my thoughts and feelings appropriately.*

- *I consider more than one possible solution to most conflict situations.*

- *I control my emotions and avoid name-calling blaming, yelling, sarcasm, nagging, withdrawing or whining.*

- *I believe my partner's needs, preferences and opinions are as important as mine.*

- *I use good communication skills when dealing with conflicts.*

There are lots of ways to solve problems. Some can be resolved with a simple request or one-minute discussion. When easy approaches don't work, consider using this method. We call it High-Trust Problem-Solving.

Marty Richards & Diana Novak

High-Trust Problem-Solving:
7 Steps To Success

1. Identify the problem, conflict or situation.

2. Clarify your needs, values and goals.

3. Assess your partner's willingness to solve the problem.

4. Find out what your partner's needs and goals are.

5. Explore possible solutions.

6. Decide what to do then do it.

7. Evaluate and refine the decision.

Here's an example of how this model can be used. We include the communication skills that help in each step.

1. Identify the problem, situation or conflict.

(Skills: Objective Description, Self-Awareness, Self-Disclosure)

Questions to ask yourself: *What's the problem? Whose problem is it? What or who is affected by the situation? Is it stated objectively and defined in the most basic terms possible?*

Example: *We have $900.00 extra this month. I want to buy a new recliner and Zola wants to put the money in savings.*

This first step is the foundation for problem-solving. Be sure you don't skip it. Both partners must agree on the objective statement, so rework it until both are satisfied that it describes the problem situation.

2. **Clarify your needs, values and goals.**

   (Skills: Self-Awareness, Self-Disclosure)

   The purpose of this step is to be as clear as possible about yourself. Ask yourself: *What's missing? What do I need, feel or want? Am I talking about a highly held value or just a preference or habit? What values are being compromised? What might happen if the situation continues? Is this an isolated situation or a symptom of a bigger or different problem?*

3. **Assess your partner's willingness to solve the problem.**

   (Skills: Question, Paraphrase, Clarify)

   Example: *Will you help me solve this problem?*

   If the answer is *yes*, go to the next step. If you get a *no*, ask...

   Would you consider... (offer a suggestion)?

   Is there anything I could do to encourage you to...?

   Do you agree there is a problem?

   Does it matter to you that this is a problem to me?

4. **Find out your partner's needs and goals.**

   (Skills: Clarify, Invite, Paraphrase, Question)

   Questions to ask your partner: *What do you need, feel, want? How does this situation affect you? What values, goals, needs, expectations or dreams are not being met?*

   Example: Ron asked, *What do you want?*

Zola said, *I need the security of money in the bank. That's more important to me than having a few crummy pieces of furniture around.*

5. **Explore possible solutions.**

    (Skills: Clear Sending and Careful Listening)

    Ask each other:

    What do you suggest?

    What do you think would work?

    How do you think we can solve it?

    Which suggestion seems to be the best, considering the needs, values and goals we've talked about?

    Then, add your own suggestions.

6. **Decide what to do then do it.**

    They agreed to put a throw over the old chair and put it in the den. They postponed buying anything new until they built up their bank account. It seemed like the responsible thing to do.

    Decide who will do what and when.
    Decide how long the trial period will be if there is one.

7. **Evaluate**

    Did it work? If not, what went wrong? What changes need to be made? Were the primary goals and needs of both of you satisfied? If not, what other issues need to be talked about later? How did the solution affect each person and the relationship?

All these steps can seem a bit overwhelming, but once you are familiar with the problem-solving model, you can get creative. Change the order of the steps, leave some out or add your own. This particular model is not as important as the mutual commitment to find a solution that satisfies you both.

> All couples should learn the art of battle as they should learn the art of making love. Good argument is objective and honest—never vicious or cruel. Good battle is healthy and constructive and brings to a relationship the principle of equal partnership.
>
> *Ann Landers*

What If Doesn't Work?

Despite your good intentions, best efforts and excellent skills, a mutually agreeable solution is not always possible. What if the problem remains? First, answer some questions:

Is the problem so important to you that you must have a solution?

Do you and your partner want a resolution but can't reach one?

Is the issue so emotional that the two of you cannot have a reasonable and respectful discussion?

Is the problem so complicated or the consequences so important that you are reluctant to risk continuing without help?

If the answer to any of these questions is *yes*, consider getting outside help such as a mediator, counselor, clergy, wise friend or trusted family member. If circumstances change, try again. Even if you don't find a solution by going through this process, there are still benefits:

You will learn…

- more about yourself and your partner.

- about your partner's willingness to cooperate.

- how important your needs are to your partner.

- there are lots of problems you can solve yourself.

- there are several good solutions to most problems.

You and Chapter 5

Now that you understand what your usual beliefs, emotions and reactions to conflict are, you can assess how well you use the skills suggested.

Problem-Solving Inventory

Decide how well these statements characterize your typical behavior when you try to solve problems with your partner.

5 = almost always true   4 = usually true   3 = true about half the time

2 = occasionally true   1 = rarely true

_____ 1. I know the difference between my opinions and the objective truth.

_____ 2. I listen with interest to opinions that differ from mine.

_____ 3. When I have a complaint or request, I ask my partner to talk it over with me.

_____ 4. When I don't understand something I ask for clarification.

_____ 5. I am willing to change my point of view when given new information.

_____ 6. I listen to criticism and complaints non-defensively.

_____ 7. I express my thoughts and feelings appropriately.

_____ 8. I consider more than one solution to most conflict situations.

_____ 9. I control my emotions and avoid name-calling, blaming, yelling, sarcasm, nagging, withdrawing or whining.

_____ 10. I believe my partner's needs, preferences and opinions are as important as my own.

_____ 11. I use good communication skills when dealing with conflicts.

_____ 12. My partner would agree with my answers to this assessment.

_____ Total Score

Add the 12 individual scores together. If your total score is close to 36 you probably have a hard time in conflict situations and your partner might not be willing to be completely honest with you. If your score is close to 50, you already have most of the skills you need to be a good problem-solver.

From this inventory, identify the items you will improve.

A Recent Conflict

Think of a recent or current conflict in your life. It can be a conflict of values or preferences. With those in mind, describe the conflict.

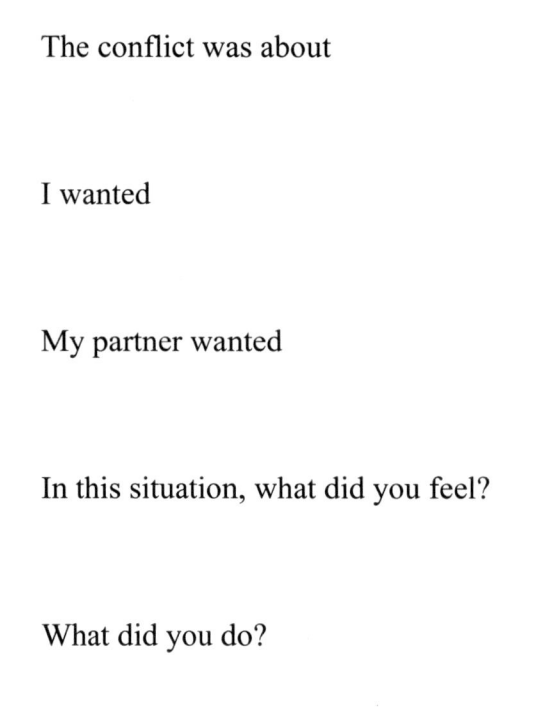

The conflict was about

I wanted

My partner wanted

In this situation, what did you feel?

What did you do?

What did your partner feel? (You might have to ask.)

What did your partner do?

Did these efforts result in a solution that satisfied both of you?

If your effort satisfied both of you, great. If not, go back through this chapter and see if you can figure out a better way to find a good solution.

We know these new beliefs and skills may seem contrived at first, but if you use them you will improve a lot of relationships. After all, aren't the possible benefits worth it?

**Oh what a tangled web we weave,
When first we practice to deceive.**

Sir Walter Scott

Marty Richards & Diana Novak

To our readers: We all make countless decisions about how to relate to others. We can spend time with people who make our lives miserable or we can seek those who enrich, respect and appreciate us. It is easy to find someone to hook up with, and it's easy to fall into relationships that just happen, but to find and keep honest, trusting and nurturing people in our lives requires conscious choices and certain characteristics, beliefs, values and skills.

We hope you will consider the ideas and skills that make it possible to know another as well as you know yourself. You can learn to understand your partner's hopes, dreams, fears and fantasies, and you can encourage your partner to know you just as completely.

The path to this kind of relationship is honesty. It doesn't guarantee intimacy, but true intimacy is not possible without it. This is an ongoing process—one that is practiced day-by-day, step-by-step, one interaction at a time. We encourage you to consider chasing this goal and sharing your life in an exciting, loving, respectful and intimate way. That is the result of a High-Trust Relationship.

> **A High-Trust Relationship is a healthy, nurturing union built on honesty, intimacy, respect and personal integrity. It is free from fear, threat and manipulation.**

Best wishes for a loving and rewarding relationship,

Marty Richards and Diana Novak